A NEW APPROACH
to
SIGHT SINGING

THIRD EDITION

A NEW APPROACH
to
SIGHT SINGING

THIRD EDITION

Sol Berkowitz
PROFESSOR OF MUSIC

Gabriel Fontrier
PROFESSOR EMERITUS OF MUSIC

Leo Kraft
PROFESSOR EMERITUS OF MUSIC

The Aaron Copland School of Music at
Queens College of the City University of New York

New York · W · W · NORTON & COMPANY · *London*

Copyright © 1960, 1976, 1986 by W. W. Norton & Company, Inc.

Music Typography by Melvin Wildberger

Layout by Ben Gamit

Library of Congress Cataloging in Publication Data

Berkowitz, Sol.
A new approach to sight singing.

1.   Sight-singing.   I.   Fontrier, Gabriel, joint
author.   II.   Kraft, Leo, joint author.   II.   Title.
MT870.B485N5   1986   784.9'4   85-28502

ISBN 0-393-95465-X

W. W. Norton & Company, Inc., 500 Fifth Avenue, New York, N.Y. 10110
W. W. Norton & Company Ltd., 10 Coptic Street, London, WCIA IPU

Printed in the United States of America

To John Castellini,
our teacher, our good friend and colleague, our editor,
this book is affectionately dedicated.

CONTENTS

ACKNOWLEDGMENTS

It is a pleasure to acknowledge the whole-hearted help and encouragement given to us, during the period in which this book was written, by our colleagues in the Queens College Music Department. Their suggestions were most stimulating and useful.

We are especially indebted to Professor John Castellini, our patient and devoted editor, who continuously labored with our manuscript and helped define its final form. Many of our basic ideas concerning music and music theory were gained during our years as students and colleagues of the late Karol Rathaus. To him, then, we owe a special debt of gratitude.

SOL BERKOWITZ
GABRIEL FONTRIER
LEO KRAFT

PREFACE
TO THE THIRD EDITION

This book consists of a coordinated body of musical material *specifically composed* for the study of sight singing. A mastery of that skill is essential to the instrumentalist, the singer, the musicologist, the composer, indeed, to any musician or intelligent amateur. Ideally, the young student should be taught sight singing from the beginning of instrumental or vocal instruction. Actually, very few students enjoy the benefits of such early training. Far too many reach an advanced level of instruction with little sight singing ability, even when their performance skills are on a professional level. Courses in sight singing, therefore, are a necessary part of the music curriculum of secondary schools, conservatories, colleges and universities.

A number of textbooks utilizing examples from the vocal and instrumental literature have been published for use in sight singing courses. *A New Approach to Sight Singing*, however, is made up entirely of music written specifically for the study of singing at sight. Exercises written for classroom use formed the basis of the First Edition of this book. Drawing upon three decades of teaching, as well as valuable comments from users of the text, we have added new material, improved some of the original exercises and written an entirely new chapter in the Third Edition.

We are convinced that our approach is pedagogically sound. We find that we are able to strike a particular level of difficulty and focus on specific problems more effectively by writing material to meet the students' needs than by using melodies drawn from the literature. Classroom experience has also shown us which types of exercise are the most useful. That experience is reflected in the revisions found in the Third Edition.

A New Approach to Sight Singing contains five chapters, as well as supplementary exercises and two appendices. The first chapter consists of unaccompanied melodies; the second, accompanied melodies; the third, vocal duets; the fourth, sets of variations; the fifth, which is new, variation sets with piano accompaniment. The supplementary exercises contain specific drills in scales and chords, chromatic notes, modes other than major and minor, whole-tone and chromatic scales, and advanced chromatic and atonal melodies. Appendix I is a glossary of musical terms found in the text. Appendix II explains some frequently used musical signs.

Each chapter is divided into four sections. Assuming two class meetings a week, each section corresponds approximately to one semester's work (thirty class hours). The material of each section is graded progressively. In every chapter, Section I consists of elementary material, Sections II and III, intermediate, and Section IV, advanced. The unit of work is the section. Section I materials in each of the five chapters make up a coordinated body of exercises to be used concurrently. The same applies to Sections II, III, and IV.

Students on the elementary level begin with the first section of each chapter. A freshman class hour might begin with singing a group of melodies (Chapter One, Section I). The class might then turn to the accompanied melodies (Chapter Two, Section I), the duets (Chapter Three, Section I), one of the variation sets (Chapter Four, Section I) or the accompanied variations (Chapter Five, Section I). It is not expected that all five chapters will be drawn upon in any one class hour. The bulk of class time will probably be devoted to singing melodies, which comprise about one half of the book. But frequent use of Chapters Two, Three, Four, and Five allows a variety of approaches to the subject, offers a desirable change of pace within the hour, and also shows the student how skills acquired in any one area may be applied to other musical situations.

A New Approach to Sight Singing is so organized that it may be adapted to various programs of study. Sections I and II, being essentially diatonic, may readily be integrated with the study of diatonic harmony and counterpoint, while Sections III and IV lend themselves to coordination with the study of advanced harmony and chromaticism.

A brief summary of each chapter offers an overview of the book's general organization:

The melodies in Chapter One encompass a variety of musical styles. These tunes are fairly short and simple, introducing technical problems gradually. To facilitate an orderly sequence of learning, the Third Edition introduces a number of topic headings. Each is followed by a short group of melodies focussed on a single topic. Immediately after, there is a longer group of melodies in which all topics presented up to that point are reviewed.

In the Third Edition the number of melodies has been increased. In addition, we have widened the scope of melodic and rhythmic types, writing many melodies with specific didactic purposes. All melodies are now edited to show phrasing and articulation clearly.

Section I of the first chapter consists of diatonic melodies, emphasizing the fundamental aspects of tonality. Stepwise motion, skips based on familiar chord outlines, and basic rhythmic patterns introduce the simplest elements in sight singing.

The melodies of Section II, while still largely diatonic, include some chromatic notes, simple modulations to the dominant or relative major, and more complex rhythms. A group of modal melodies concludes this section.

Section III includes melodies with more chromaticism and additional modulations. Melodies are longer, phrase structures more diverse, and rhythms more complex.

In Section IV, the exercises present more challenging problems in tonality, rhythm, meter, phrase structure, dynamics, and musical interpretation. The section concludes with a group of melodies based on twentieth-century idioms.

The treble, alto and bass clefs are used in all sections; the tenor clef is introduced in Section IV. From one melody to the next the student will encounter changes of clef, key, mode, meter, tempo, dynamics, phrasing, rhythm, and musical style. Some melodies embody the expansive contour of the Baroque; some are in the Classical style; others demonstrate nineteenth-century chromaticism; many are derived from the language of folk and popular music, as well as jazz.

Experience has strengthened our conviction that the piano is an invaluable aid for developing musicianship. By playing while singing the student improves intonation, develops rhythm skills and learns much about the harmonic implications of melody. In the Third Edition, Chapter Two, Sing and Play, has been augmented considerably. In particular, a number of exercises based on simple chord patterns will be found in the first half of this chapter. We have also written a new Chapter Five, consisting of Themes and Variations for Voice and Piano. This chapter widens the scope of sing and play exercises, offering a substantial body of graded material with varied piano parts. The short exercises of Chapter Five afford many changes of pace which can help maintain the level of interest during a class hour. Sing and Play exercises in Chapters Two and Five need not be performed at sight; they are particularly valuable as prepared assignments.

The purpose of the Chapter Three, Duets, is to develop skill in ensemble singing. The student must not only sing one part correctly, but must do so while listening to another part. Chapter Three has been expanded and re-edited. In addition, we have added more simple duets in Sections I and II. We have also found that the duets, beyond their value as sung exercises, are adaptable to dictation in two parts.

Themes and Variations, Chapter Four, provide the experience of singing relatively extended compositions while emphasizing various problems of musical interpretation. Because the character of the melodies changes from one variation to another, the student is stimulated to develop a sensitive performance technique. This chapter has been completely re-edited.

All chapters afford many opportunities for practice in building rhythm skills of the most diverse nature on graded levels of increasing difficulty.

The Supplementary Exercises provide a large variety of materials designed as drills in intervallic relationships, intonation and rhythm. Part One of the Supplementary Exercises is to be used with Sections I and II of the five chapters, while Part Two is to be used with Sections III and IV.

Everyone can learn to sing. Whether or not one possesses a beautiful voice, competence in sight singing can be achieved by consistent study. Good sight singing is a developed ability that can be acquired through diligent practice. The satisfaction thus gained will more than justify the effort and time expended. Sight singing is certainly not an end in itself, but it is one of the necessary tools which any competent musician must possess. Music does not live on paper. To bring it to life there must be an instrument that can sing, an ear that can hear, and a sensitive musical mind that can sing and hear in the silence of thought.

****

We take this opportunity to express our appreciation and thanks to the many generations of Queens College students whose reactions to our book have helped shape our thinking and who have taught us so much. Beyond that, the widespread positive response to the first two editions has encouraged us to continue our search for as many new approaches to sight singing as we can create.

Berkowitz/Fontrier/Kraft
Queens College, 1986

A NEW APPROACH
to
SIGHT SINGING

THIRD EDITION

Chapter One

MELODIES

Before singing a melody (or performing music of any sort) it is necessary to understand thoroughly the system of music notation we use today. The five-line staff with the clef signs, time signatures, tempo indications, and expression markings constitute a music code, all the elements of which must be decoded simultaneously in order to transform into meaningful music what has been set down on paper.

ESTABLISH THE KEY

The melodies in Section I are tonal. Each is written in a specific key and the student must establish that key before attempting to sing. The tonic note of the key (rather than the first note of the melody) should be played on the piano or the pitch pipe and sung by the student. Then the scale of the key should be sung, ascending and descending, after which an arpeggio consisting of tonic, third, fifth, and octave may be sung to establish further a feeling for the tonality of the melody.

ESTABLISH THE TEMPO

Next it is necessary to take cognizance of the tempo (rate of speed) and the meter (number of beats to the measure). Many different tempo indications have been used in this book to familiarize the student with most of the terms in common use. It is important that the singer know the meaning of these tempo markings, all of which are to be found in the Glossary (page 315).

The time signature denotes meter. Simple meters (duple, triple, and quadruple) are indicated by signatures having a 2, 3, or 4 as the upper numeral, or by the signs $\mathbf{C}$ (corresponding to $\frac{4}{4}$ meter) or $\mathbf{\mathfrak{C}}$ (*alla breve*, corresponding to $\frac{2}{2}$ meter). Regular compounded meters ($\frac{6}{8}$, $\frac{9}{8}$, and $\frac{12}{8}$) are combinations of simple meters within one measure.

Tempo can be established and meter defined by the student if he beats time as a conductor does. Standard conducting patterns should be used consistently. $\frac{6}{8}$ time may be conducted in six or in two beats; $\frac{9}{8}$ and $\frac{12}{8}$ time in separate beats or in three or four beats respectively. Tempo, and often the character of a melody, will serve the student in determining how to conduct compound meters.

SINGING MELODIES WITHOUT TEXTS

It is advisable to sing some definite syllable for every note the better to control quality and intonation. In many foreign countries *solfeggio* (the application of the *sol-fa* syllables to the degrees of the scale) is used in sight singing. This practice is officially sanctioned by foreign national conservatories. In our country, however, several methods of singing melodies without texts are in common use. These may be summarized as follows:

Fixed Do
In the fixed *Do* system, our notes, C, D, E, F, G, A, and B, are called *Do, Re, Mi, Fa, Sol, La,* and *Ti.* In singing a melody, the name for

each note is sung without regard to any accidental. Countries which use this technique have been quite successful with it, perhaps because of the rigorous early training which their students receive.

Movable Do

In the movable *Do* system, *Do* always represents the tonic or first degree of the scale, regardless of key. Accidentals are accounted for by changing the syllables. The ascending chromatic scales reads as follows:

Do, Di, Re, Ri, Mi, Fa, Fi, Sol, Si, La, Li, Ti, Do

The descending chromatic scale reads as follows:

Do, Ti, Te, La, Le, Sol, Se, Fa, Mi, Me, Re, Ra, Do

When a melody modulates, the new tonic is called *Do*, and the other notes of the scale are renamed accordingly. The purpose of this system is to emphasize the relationship between the degrees of the scale, and to develop a feeling for tonality even when the tonal center shifts.

Other Methods

Numbers (1, 2, 3, etc.) may be used instead of syllables (*Do, Re, Mi*, etc.). The application is the same as in the movable *Do* system except that there is no numeral change for chromatic tones.

One syllable, such as *la*, may be used for all pitches. Thus the singer does not have to translate the pitch names into syllables or numbers.

A musician is expected to know the system in common use wherever he may be; therefore, the student should master more than one of these techniques.

PHRASING

The student is urged to avoid note-to-note singing and to make a genuine effort to grasp an entire phrase as a musical entity. To guide and encourage this process of looking ahead, slurs and articulation markings have been placed over the phrases of every melody. These indications define the phrase structure and serve as a guide to breathing.

MUSICAL VALUES

In practicing the singing of melodies, as in practicing an instrument, the beginner may be tempted to concentrate on producing the correct pitch, hoping that other musical values will be acquired in due course. But melodies do not exist without rhythm; they also have nuances of dynamics and tempo, and climaxes. These qualities are an integral part of the music. It is possible to improve one's musicianship while learning the technique of sight singing by thinking about musical values with the first melody in the book. As an aid to intelligent and sensitive performance we have included dynamics, expression, and articulation markings throughout the book. The eye should be trained to observe them; the mind to implement them.

Clearly, there is much to do, and it is suggested that the student *make haste slowly*. The first melodies should be studied carefully in order to develop good musical habits. The student should sing a melody several times, if necessary, until ease and fluency are achieved.

4

MELODIES *Section I*

To be used with Section I of all other Chapters

The first melodies emphasize the basic aspects of tonality. They are designed to include easily recognizable scale and chordal patterns. These diatonic melodies are based upon both major and minor modes.

The phrases are usually symmetrical and short enough to be grasped at a glance. However, the diversity of rhythms, keys, modes, tempos, dynamics, and clefs should provide a variety of musical experiences. The alto clef is introduced in exercise 41b; compound meter $\frac{6}{8}$ in 73c; the minor mode in 57.

Students who are unfamiliar with one or another of the clefs that are used in this section should prepare for the actual singing by reciting the names of the notes in strict time. Then the melody should be sung, again naming the notes. To develop facility in reading the various clefs, the student should also *play* the melodies which have been sung in class.

The first seventeen melodies are based entirely on stepwise motion.

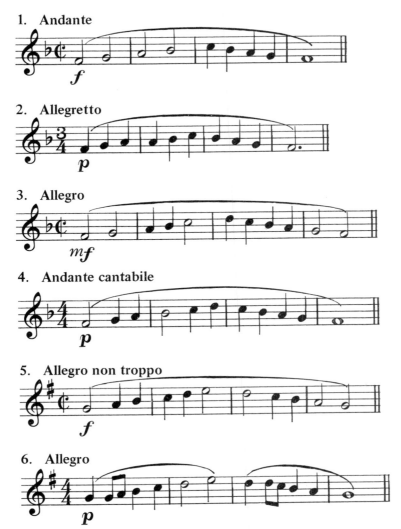

7. **Allegretto**

8. **Andante**

The next four melodies are in five-measure phrases.

9. **Largo**

10. **Andantino**

11. **Allegro**

12. **Allegretto**

13. **Allegro**

14. **Con moto**

15. **Allegretto**

16. **Allegro**

17. **Allegro deciso**

The following eleven melodies emphasize skips in the tonic triad.

18. **Allegro**

19. **Andante con moto**

20. **Vivace**

21. **Allegro moderato**

22. **Allegro con brio**

23. **Andante cantabile**

24. **Allegretto**

25. Presto

26. Allegro

27. Allegretto

28. Andante

29. Andante

The rhythm ♩. ♪ is introduced in the next six melodies.

30. Allegro moderato

31. Allegro

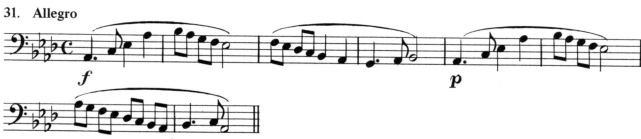

32. Vivace

33. Andante

34. Andante cantabile

35. Andante

36. Andante con moto

37. Allegretto

38. Tempo di menuetto

39. Vivace

40. Andante cantabile

The same melody written with three different clefs.

41a. Moderato

41b. Moderato

41c. Moderato

The next twelve melodies are written with the alto clef.

42. Andante

43. Largo

44. Allegretto

45. Allegro con spirito

46. Con moto

56. Allegro con spirito

Three C-minor scales

Natural

Harmonic

Melodic

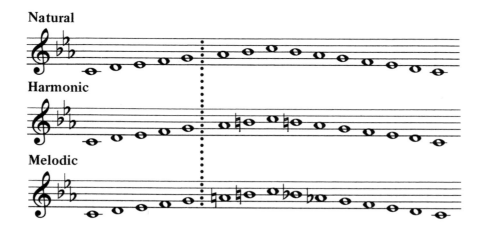

Melodies in which the major and minor modes are compared may be found in *Supplementary Exercises*, p. 294.

The next seven melodies are based on minor triads.

57. Andante

58. Allegro

59. Andantino

The following eight melodies include skips in the tonic minor triad.

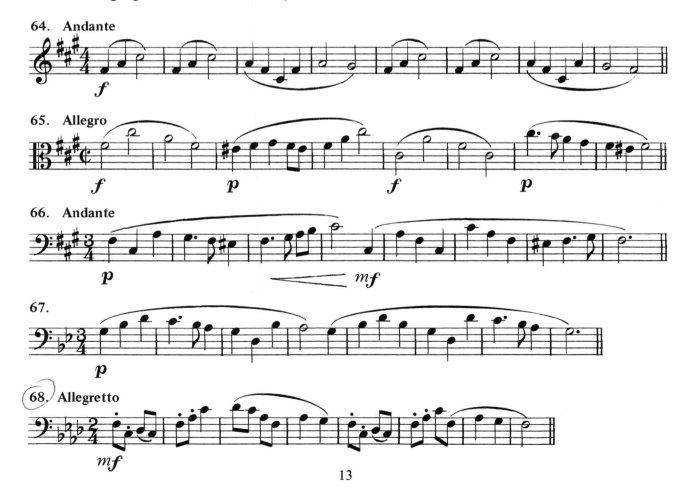

69. Andante espressivo

70. Moderato

71. Andante con moto

72. Allegretto

The same melody notated in three different meters.

73a. Moderato

73b. Allegro

73c. Larghetto

The next nine melodies are in $\frac{6}{8}$ time.

74. Andantino

75. Andantino

Rests are included in melodies from this point.

86. **Allegro moderato**

87. **Andante cantabile**

88. **Allegro**

89. **Andantino**

90. **Allegro**

The next three melodies begin with the 5th of the tonic triad.

91. **Allegro**

92. **Larghetto**

93. **Andante**

94. **Moderato**

95. **Andante pastorale**

96. **Lento**

The next three melodies begin with the 3rd of the tonic triad.

97. **Allegro**

98. **Andantino**

99. **Allegro con spirito**

100. **Andante**

101. Frisch und munter

102. Allegretto

The next six melodies begin with ♩ upbeats.

103. Allegro moderato

104. Andantino

105. Tempo di menuetto

106. Allegro deciso

107. Andantino

108. Tempo di menuetto

The next eight melodies include skips in the IV chord.

109. Andante

110. Andante

111. Allegro

112. Allegro

113. Larghetto

114. Larghetto

115. Allegro energico

116. Allegro energico

117. Allegro

sempre *p* e leggiero

133. **Bewegt**

134. **Allegro**

135. **Comodo**

136. **Assez lent**

The rhythm ♫ is included in the next six melodies.

137. **Larghetto**

138. **Allegro deciso**

139. **Langsam**

The next six melodies include skips in the V chord.

164. Adagietto

165. Valse

MELODIES   *Section II*

To be used with Section II of all other Chapters

These melodies contain simple modulations, more complex rhythms, and diatonic skips in a variety of contexts. As in Melodies, Section I, the tonality of each melody is clearly defined. Some phrases are longer; some less sym-metrical; syncopations are introduced; and the vocal range is extended.

A group of modal melodies begins with 298.

The following six melodies include skips in the V⁷ chord.

27

177. **Andante espressivo**

178. **Adagietto**

179. **Con moto**

180. **Allegretto**

181. **Ballando**

The next five melodies include the time signatures $\frac{3}{8}$, $\frac{9}{8}$, $\frac{12}{8}$, and $\frac{6}{4}$.

182. **Andante cantabile**

183. **Doux et expressif**

184. Larghetto

185. Pastorale

186. Andante con moto

The following three melodies include triplets.

187. Maestoso

188. Largo

189. Andante con moto

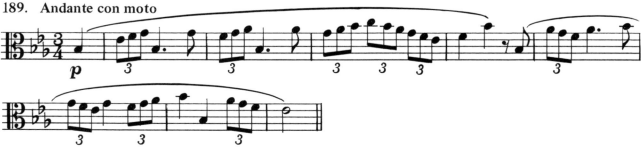

190. **Andante**

191. **Ziemlich schnell**

Skips of all diatonic intervals are included in the next four melodies.

192. **Andante con moto**

193. **Lentement**

194. **Langsam**

Ties are introduced in the next five melodies.

205. Andante

The next ten melodies include the upbeats ♪, ♫ and ♬ .

206. Andante

207. Allegro marziale

208. Andante pastorale

209. Allegro grazioso

The next eight melodies include syncopations.

216. **Allegro**

217. **Sustained**

218. **Gaio**

219. **Largo**

220. **Andante cantabile**

221. **Lively**

222. **Brisk**

223. Allegro

224. Andante

225. Allegro moderato   (Var. V of 5th *Theme and Variations*,   p. 232)

226. Andantino

227. Andante

234. **Ländler**

235. **Andantino grazioso**

236. **Valse**

237. **Un poco sostenuto**

The next six melodies include chromatic neighbor notes.

238. **Andante**

239. **Andante**

240. **Allegretto** (Var. V of 7th *Theme and Variations*, **p. 235**)

241. **Andantino piacevole**

242. **Allegro molto**

243. **Allegretto**

244. **Allegro energico**

245. Mässig und zart

246. Allegro deciso

247. Lively

248. Moderato con moto

249. Andantino

250. **Lively**

251. **Allegretto**

252. **Cheerful**

The following six melodies introduce modulation to the relative major of the minor mode.

253. **Allegro**

259. Andante espressivo

260. Allegro

261. Gaily

262. Andante

263. Waltz tempo

The next three melodies include chromatic passing notes.

268. **Moderato con moto**

269. **Andante con moto**

270. **Allegro non troppo**

271. **Lilting**

272. **Ben ritmico**

278. **Con moto**

279. **Andante con moto**

280. **Andante sostenuto**

The next four melodies include modulation to the dominant.

281. **Allegretto grazioso**

282. **Assez vite**

283. Fanfare

284. Allegro assai

285. Allegro e ben marcato

286. Allegro gioviale

287. Andantino

288. Allegro moderato

289. Minuet

290. Andante ed espressivo

291. Modéré

292. Allegro gioviale

293. Briskly

294. Etwas gedehnt

295. Largo

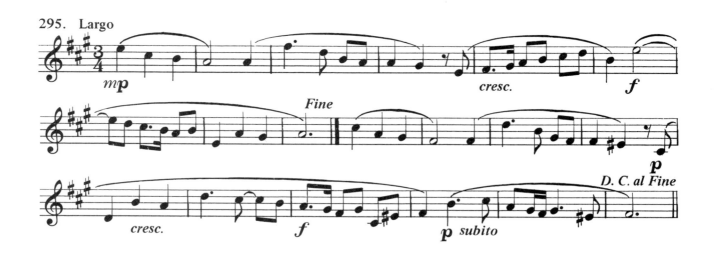

296. Allegro lunatico

297. Scherzando

Modal melodies based on the following four modes.

MELODIES   *Section III*

To be used with Section III of all other Chapters

Chromatic alterations are used with increasing frequency in the melodies of this section. Some indicate modulation; some are factors in secondary dominant harmonies; others are melodic embellishments. Within these melodies there is an increasing diversity of rhythms, intervals, phrase structures, and musical styles.

The material of Section III can readily be correlated with the study of chromatic harmony.

Skips larger than one octave are found in the next four melodies.

314. **Allegro**

315. **Allegro moderato**

316. **Andante con moto**

317. **Allegro deciso**

323. **Mit Kraft**

324. **Allegro gioviale**

325. **Valse**

326. **Allegro grazioso**

Skips to chromatic notes are introduced in the next five melodies.

327. **Allegro moderato**

328. **Andante mosso**

329. **Adagio espressivo e rubato**

330. **Andante espressivo**

331. **Largo con affetto**

332. **Allegretto grazioso (Theme of 13th *Theme and Variations*, p. 242)**

333. **Larghetto**

334. Allegretto

335. Andante

336. Moderato

337. Gavotte

338. Pas trop lent

344. Allegretto

345. Well accented

346. Ballando

347. Sostenuto ed espressivo

357. Briskly

mf staccato

cresc. poco a poco

ff

358. Spiritoso

f

più f

p subito — *f*

359. Tempo di valse

p

Secondary dominants are outlined in the next five melodies.

360. Energetic

f

361. Andante con moto

p

362. Allegro

363. Sehr rasch

364. Allegretto

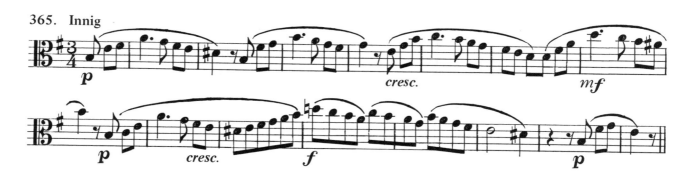

365. Innig

366. Allegro con spirito

The meters $\frac{5}{8}$ and $\frac{5}{4}$ are introduced in the next five melodies.

372. Allegro

373. Andantino

374. Allegro

375. Slowly and simply

376. Moderate

377. Lento

378. Larghetto

379. Presto

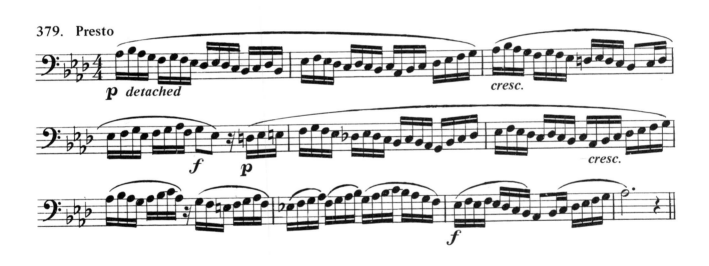

380. Lilting

381. Andantino amabile

382. Lebhaft

383. Allegretto

384. Animé et très expressif

389. Medium bounce

390. Andante espressivo

391. Rather slowly

392. Vif et léger

393. Modéré et doucement

The following four melodies, in the major mode, include the flatted sixth scale degree.

394. **Andante**

395. **Andantino**

396. **Waltz**

397. **Andante semplice**

398. **Mässig und einfach**

399. **Quasi presto**

400. Allegro giocoso

401. Allegretto

402. Tarantella

403. Allegro gioviale

The dominant 9th chord is outlined in the next five melodies.

404. Andante

405. Larghetto

411. **Largo**

412. **Allegretto scherzoso**

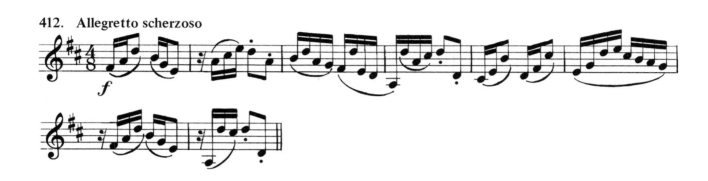

413. **Largo**

414. **Allegretto**

415. Langsam, mit Empfindung

416. Vif

417. Lebhaft

418. Ballando

419. Allegretto e leggiero

420. Galop

421. Lento assai

422. Fast

423. **Lento ed espressivo**

424. **Allegretto**

425. **Il più presto possibile**

426. **Valse**

427. Alla marcia

428. Andante e rubato

429. Allegro molto

430. Animated

436. In jig time

437. Allegro assai

438. Mässig und ausdrucksvoll

444. Andantino

445. Presto

446. Larghetto

MELODIES   *Section IV*

To be used with Section IV of all other Chapters

The melodies in this section present interesting problems of intonation, rhythm, and phrase structure. The tenor clef is introduced at the beginning of the section. Modulation to remote keys, the use of augmented and diminished intervals, a more intensified chromaticism, modal idioms, and complex syncopation offer the advanced student both challenge and stimulus.

The concluding melodies of this section introduce 20th-century melodic idioms.

The next nine melodies are written using the tenor clef.

447. Allegro

448. Moderato

449. Largo

85

456. Vivace (Theme of 17th *Theme and Variations*, p. 248)

457. Lento

458. Minuet

459. Tempo di valzer

460. Doux, mais avec mouvement

461. Andantino

462. Con spirito

463. Lento

464. Con moto

465. Allegretto

466. Lento

467. Valse brillante

468. Molto adagio

469. Andantino

470. Slow and expressive

471. Andante

477. **Langsam und ausdrucksvoll**

478. **Allegro energico**

479. **Allegro assai**

The flatted supertonic scale degree is introduced in the next four melodies.

480. **Andante**

481. **Allegro**

487. Larghetto

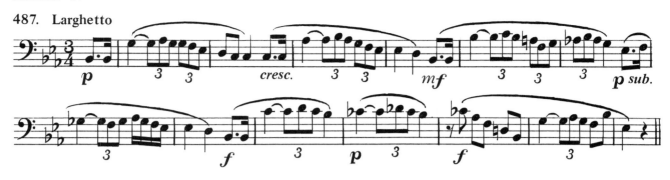

488. Allegretto

489. Con anima

490. Langsam und zart

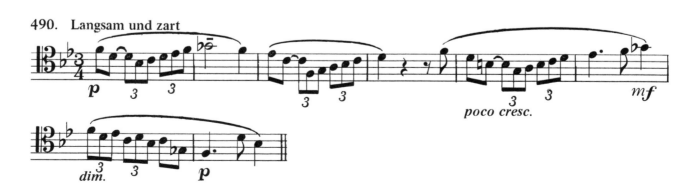

491. Lively

492. Allegretto

493. Alla marcia

494. Arioso—Andante cantabile

495. Allegretto

496. Lively

497. Adagio

498. Allegretto

499. Larghetto

500. Andante con moto

501. Waltz

502. Andante con moto

503. Free and easy

504. Ländler

505. Valse brillante

506. Moderato

507. Etwas gedehnt

508. Allegro

509. Allegro deciso

510. Arietta–Andante

511. With movement

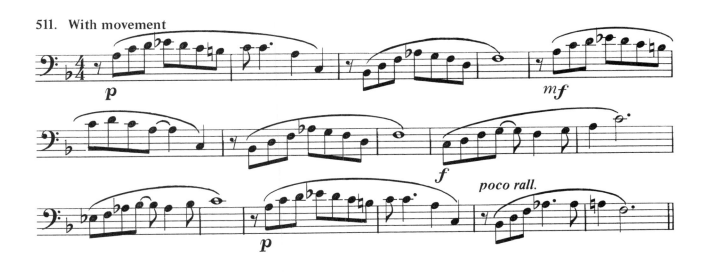

512. Allegro

513. Briskly

514. Grave

515. Lento

516. Doux et lentement

517. Lento ed espressivo

518. Allegro piacevole

The next five melodies include changing meters.

519. Allegro

520. Langsam

521. Andante

532. Allegro

533. Andante cantabile

534. Valse triste

535. Maestoso

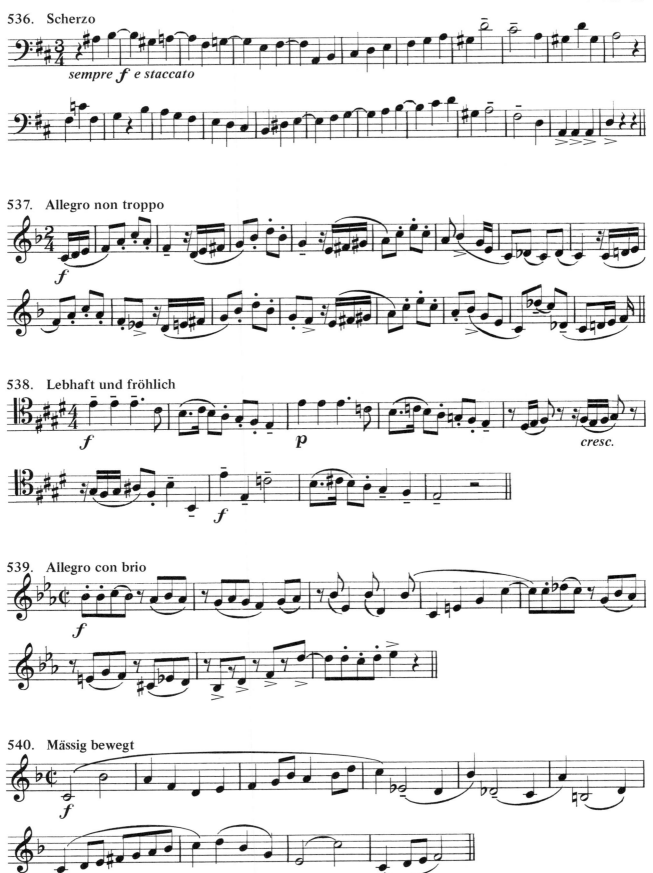

550. Mazurka--Risoluto

551. Slowly, expressively

552. Andantino

553. With a well-marked rhythm

554. Presto

555. Tempo di marcia

Major and minor modes are combined in the next seven melodies.

556. Allegro con spirito

557. Allegretto

558. Bewegt

559. Allegro

560. Modéré et doux

561. Allegro non tanto

562. Tempo di minuetto

563. **Expansively**

564. **Vif**

565. **Andantino**

566. **Andante e semplice**

567. Mässig und zart

568. Vivo

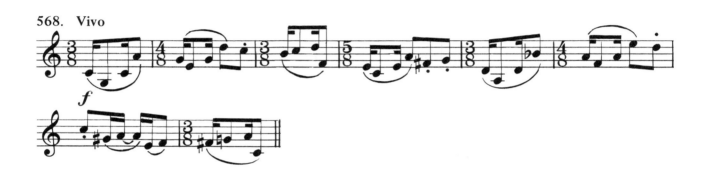

569. Con moto

570. With spirit

571. Lively

f *la seconda volta* *p*

p

572. Spiritoso

f

p

f

573. Un poco pesante

f

p cresc. molto

ff *mf*

f

574. Lebhaft und stark

f

zurückhalten

im Zeitmass

p

ff

575. Andante espressivo

The next six melodies feature the interval of a perfect 4th.

576. Allegro

577. Moderato

578. Mässig

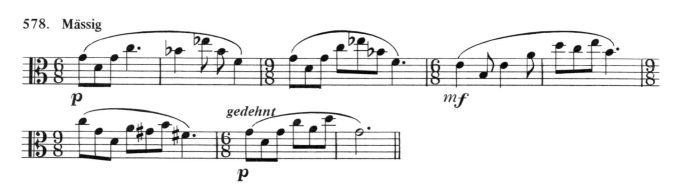

583. Allegro marcato

584. Andante

585. Allegro giocoso

586. Andante

587. Moderato

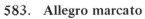

116

The next three melodies are based on octatonic scales.

592. Vivo

593. Allegro con brio

Chapter Two

SING AND PLAY

These exercises are designed to provide an introductory experience in sight singing vocal music with piano accompaniment. The piano will be especially useful in overcoming potential difficulties with intonation.

These little pieces should be sung and played by the same person. Therefore the piano parts have been kept at a minimal level of difficulty. The emphasis is on the melodic line and its relationship to the accompaniment. Students with little pianistic ability may use the duets of Chapter Three as additional easy sing and play exercises.

The skill acquired through the study of this chapter will prepare the student to explore some of the richest treasures in the musical literature.

SING AND PLAY   *Section I*

1. Moderato

2. Andante

3. Moderato

4. Moderato

120

1 to 19

20. Allegretto

21. Allegro

22. Moderato

23. Andante

24a. Andante (maggiore)

24b. Andante (minore)

25a. Andantino (maggiore)

25b. Andantino (minore)

26. Allegretto

27. Moderato

28. Moderato

29. Allegro

30a. Moderato (maggiore)

30b. Moderato (minore)

31. Allegretto

32a. Allegro (maggiore)

32b. Allegro (minore)

33. **Brightly**

SING AND PLAY   *Section II*

41b. Moderato (minore)

42. Andante

43. Moderato

44a. Allegro (maggiore)

44b. Allegro (minore)

45a. Modéré (maggiore)

45b. Modéré (minore)

46. Allegro

47a. Moderato (maggiore)

47b. **Moderato (minore)**

48. **Allegretto**

49. **Lento**

50. Allegro

51a. Andantino (maggiore)

51b. Andantino (minore)

52. Andante

53. Moderato

54. Moderato

55. Allegretto

56. Moderato

57. Allegretto

58. Lento

59. Allegro ma non troppo

60. Andante

61. Adagio

62. Allegro

63. Allegro

64. Lento

65. Langsam

66. Andante

140

67. Andante

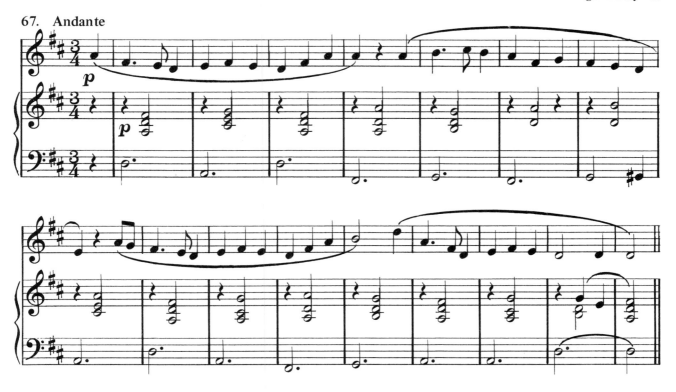

68. Moderato

69. Adagio

70. Andante cantabile

71. Allegretto

72. Adagietto

73. Alla marcia

The first five pitch-es of all three mi-nor scales are not wick-ed witch-es from scar-y fair-y tales. Do re *may* fa sol *la ti* do do re *may* fa sol *lay tay* do do re *may* fa sol *lay ti* do *lay ti* do We end the mel-o-dic mi-nor *la ti* do We end the na-tu-ral mi-nor *lay tay* do, ain't it so? The first five pitch-es, same for all three. Now we sing that old har-mon-ic, we're home free!

SING AND PLAY   *Section III*

74a. **Allegro assai (maggiore)**

74b. **Allegro assai (minore)**

75. **Allegretto**

76. Lento

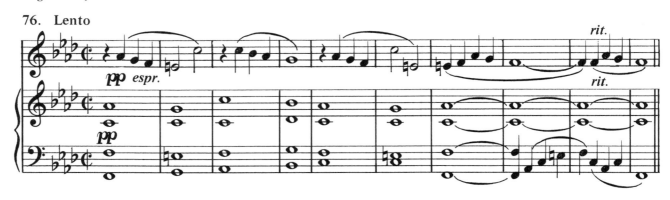

77. Andantino

78. Andante con moto

79. **Allegretto grazioso**

80. **Largo**

81. **Allegretto**

82a.   Moderato (maggiore)

82b.   Moderato (minore)

83. Pastorale

84. Etwas bewegt

85. Mässig und zart

86. Andantino

Appoggiatura: see *Glossary*.

87. Doux et expressif

88. Langsam

89. Recitativo

90. Slowly

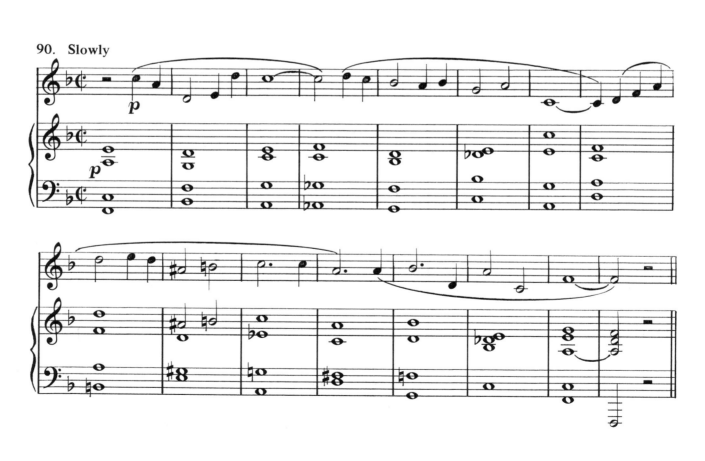

91. **Moderately fast**

92. **Larghetto**

93. Berceuse

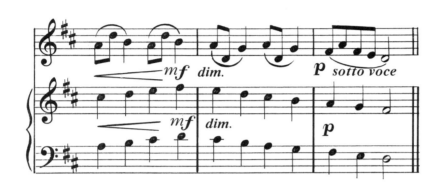

94. Mässig und ausdrucksvoll

95. Andante maestoso

96. Andantino

97. Andante cantabile

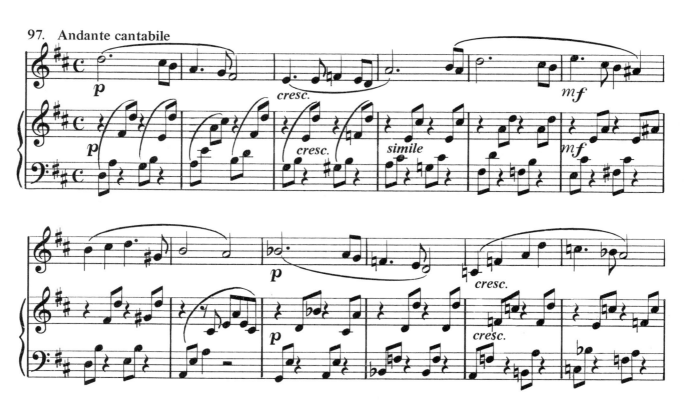

98. Allegretto

99. Recitativo

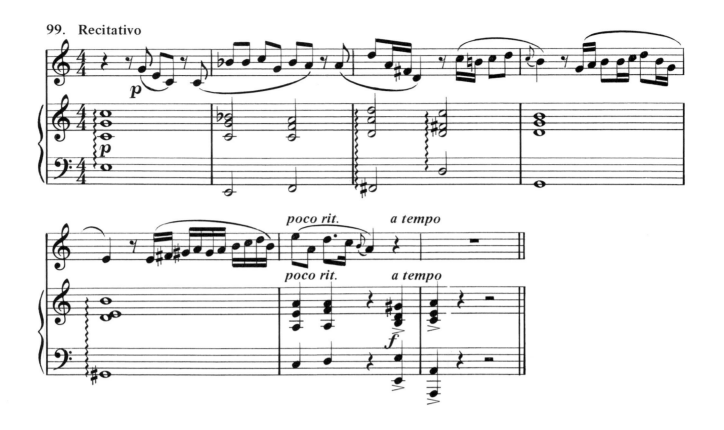

100. Recitativo ed arioso

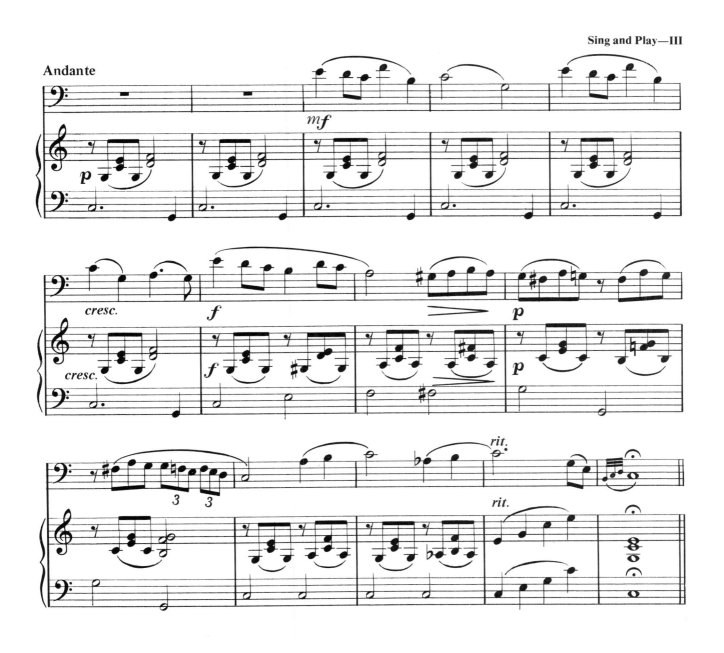

Andante

101. Fast and peppy

To - mor-row I must play and sing as

if I can do ev-'ry-thing, I prac-ticed hard the whole night through!

slowly   *rit.*   *with more conviction, slowly*

But, but, *boo!* It must be re-al-ized! My voice and fin-gers must be syn-chro-nized.

slowly   *rit.*   *colla voce*

dim. poco a poco

a tempo   *p*

Be-ware, be-ware,   take care, take care,

p

rit.   *a tempo*   *f*

take care, take care, Do not ad-mit to an-y de-spair, Cour-age gets me there

rit.   *a tempo*

f

SING AND PLAY   *Section IV*

102. Innig

103. Andante sostenuto

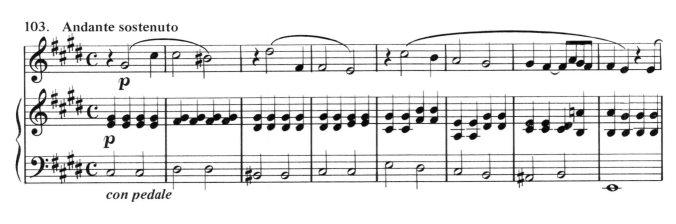

con pedale

104. Mit Empfindung

105. Moderato

106. Moderately fast

107. Jazz waltz ♩ = 60

con pedale

108. Tempo di valzer

109. Vivo

110. Andante con moto

111. Ziemlich langsam

112. Lento

113. Pastorale

114. Slowly

115. **Con calore**

rall.

116. **Andantino con grazia**

117. Largo

118. Allegro con brio

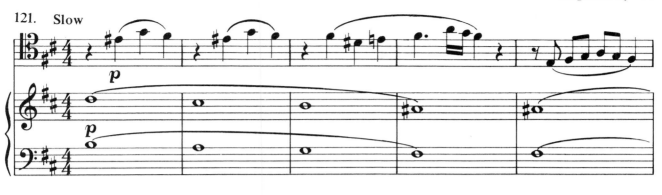

121. Slow

122. Doux et expressif

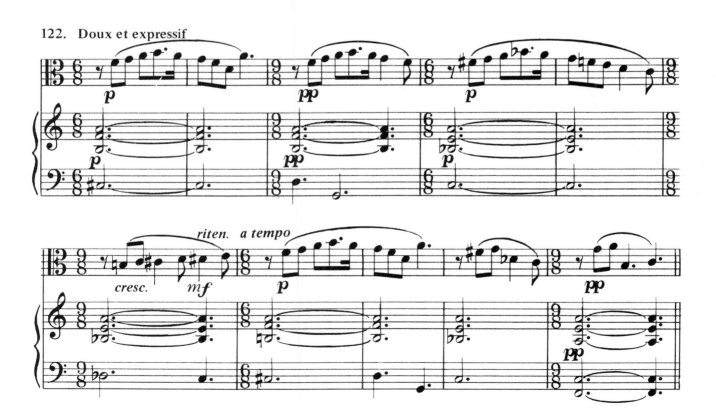

123. Tenderly

124. Moderately slow

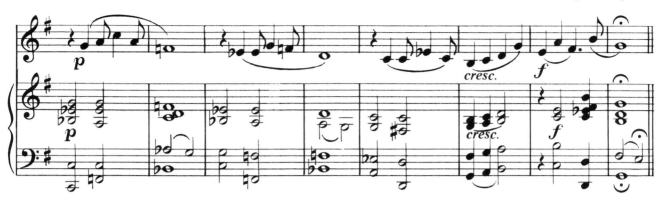

125. Ziemlich langsam

126. Con calma

127. Andante con moto

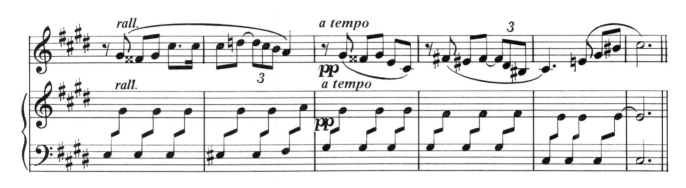

128. **Energetic, not too fast**

129. Teneramente

130. Slowly

131. Slow and expressive

132. Jazz waltz

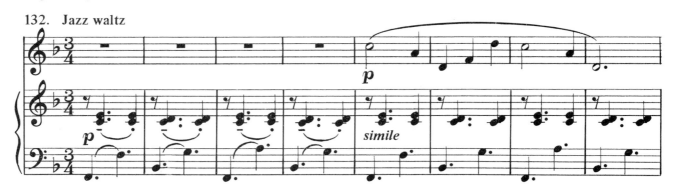

133. Andantino

134. Doux et expressif

135. Molto sostenuto

136. Modéré

137. Lentement

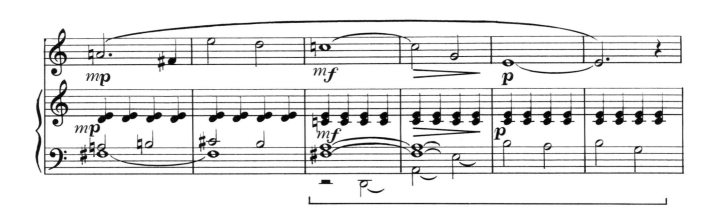

138. Ruhig ♩ = 60

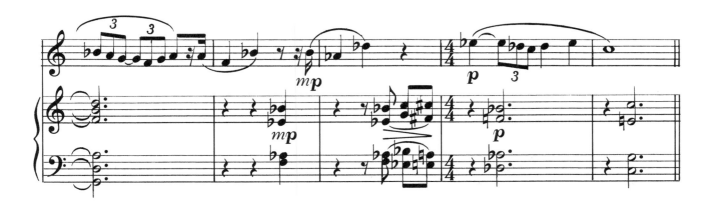

139. Langsam ♩ = 54

140. Andantino espressivo

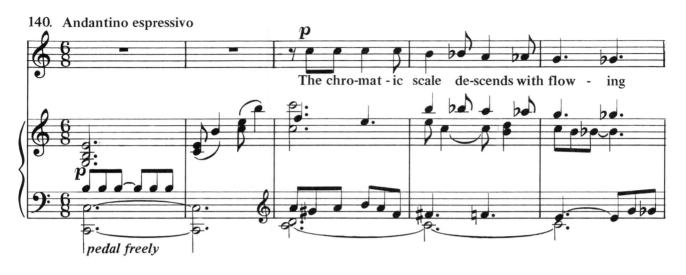

The chro-mat-ic scale de-scends with flow - ing

pedal freely

ease, So, please,___ en - joy ev-'ry mo-ment. All be - long to one

meno mosso
più p
morendo

song,___ just one love-ly song.___

Chapter Three

DUETS

The experience of singing one part while listening to another develops that sense of independence so essential to a good ensemble performer. Hearing the harmonic and contrapuntal relation between your melodic line and another will help maintain correct intonation and rhythmic precision. For additional practice, it is useful to play one part at the piano while singing the other.

DUETS   *Section I*

1. **Andante**

2. **Allegretto**

3. **Lento**

4. **Andantino**

5. **Larghetto**

6. **Andante**

7. **Larghetto**

8. **Allegretto**

9. **Andante**

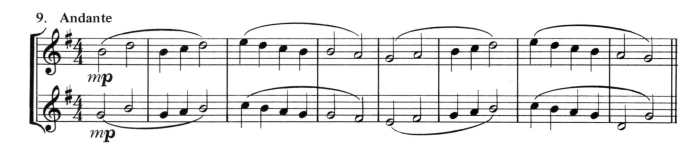

10. **Allegro**

11. Allegretto

12. Andante

13. Allegretto

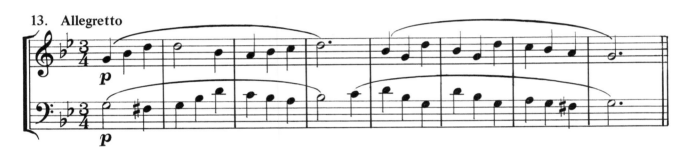

14. Moderato con moto

15. Andante

16. Andante cantabile

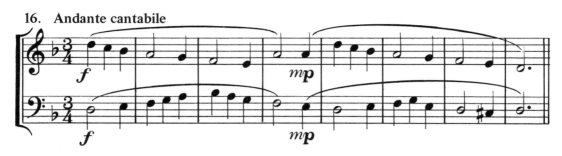

17. Larghetto

18. Allegro moderato

19. Allegretto

20. Allegro

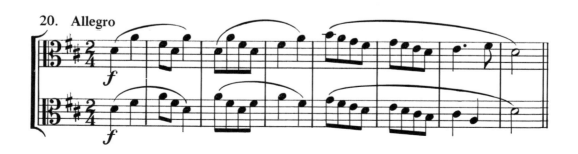

21. Allegro con spirito

22. Moderato con moto

23. Allegro giocoso

24. Allegro

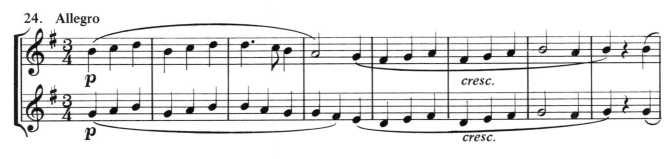

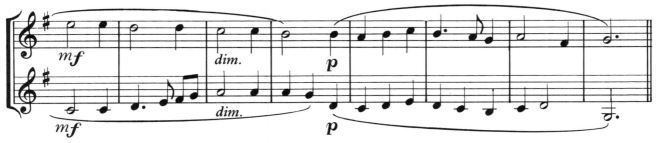

25. Allegretto

26. Allegro moderato

27. Allegretto

28. Lento

29. Andante espressivo

30. Allegretto

31. Andante con moto

DUETS *Section II*

35. **Andantino**

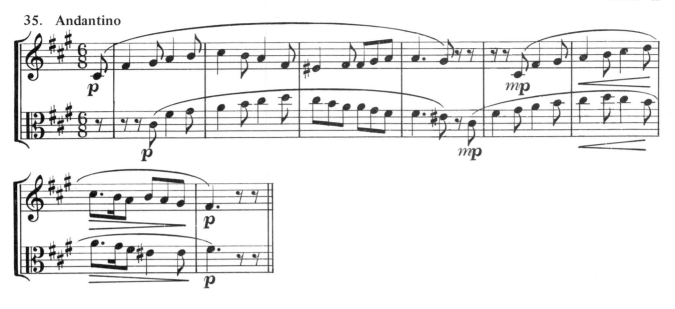

36. **Langsam**

37. **Largo espressivo**

38. Lento

39. Andante espressivo

40. Giocoso

41. **Mässig**

42. **Allegro con spirito**

43. **Andantino**

44. En allant

45. Andante cantabile

46. Allegretto giocoso

51. **Andante con moto**

52. **Flowing**

53. **Allegro**

58. Allegretto

59. Con brio

60. Larghetto

61. **Andante con moto**

62. **Andantino (Mixolydian)**

63. **Sustained and expressive (Mixolydian)**

64. **Andantino (Dorian)**

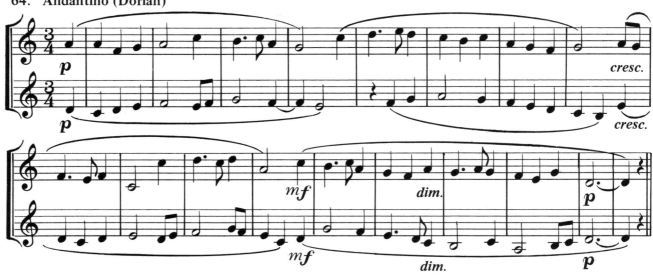

65. **Ben ritmico (Phrygian)**

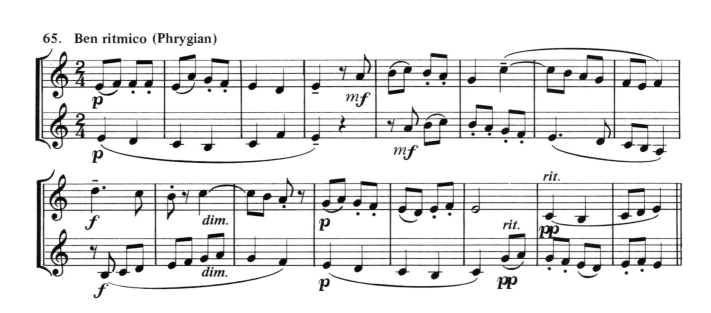

DUETS *Section III*

66. Moderately fast

69. Allegretto piacevole

70. Gedehnt

71. Vivo

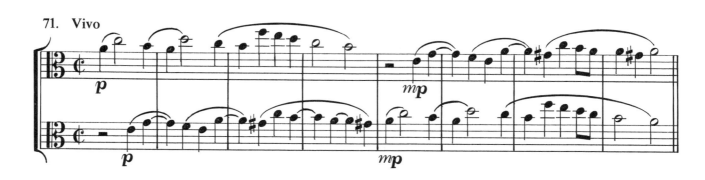

72. Allegro

73. Langsam

74. Andante con moto

75. Vivo

76. Allegro non troppo

77. Molto allegro

81. Allegro moderato

82. Deciso

83. Spiritoso

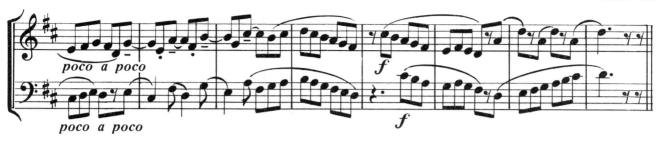

84. Allegretto

85. Adagietto

86. Langsam und ausdrucksvoll

87. Largo

88. Lento

89. Andante affettuoso

90. Langsam und ausdrucksvoll

91. Allegro molto

DUETS *Section IV*

92. Allegro deciso

93. Moderately fast

94. Mässig

95. Etwas langsam

96. Allegro

97. Affettuoso

98. Allegro deciso

99. Comodo

100. Adagio non tanto

101. Andante con moto

102. Adagietto

105. Ziemlich langsam

106. Andante con moto

107. Gedehnt

108. **Andante**

109. **Andante espressivo**

110. Molto lento

111. Deciso

112. Allegretto e marcato

113. March

114. Allegro

Chapter Four

THEMES AND VARIATIONS

Themes and variations provide the opportunity of singing more extended musical compositions. The constantly changing character of the music as the variations unfold demands a larger range of interpretive skills than the shorter melodies of Chapter One.

The nature of the material and the levels of difficulty are comparable to those of the melodies in Chapter One.

THEMES AND VARIATIONS   *Section I*

1st Theme and Variations

2nd Theme and Variations

Theme: Moderato

Var. I: Andante

Var. II: Allegro

Var. III: Presto

Var. IV: Lento

Var. V: Allegro con brio

3rd Theme and Variations

Theme: Andante

4th Theme and Variations

Theme: Andantino

Var. I: L'istesso tempo

Var. II: Un poco allegro

Var. III: Allegretto

Var. IV (Minore): Lento

Var. V (Maggiore): Allegro giocoso

5th Theme and Variations

Theme: Allegro moderato

Var. I: Allegro

Var. II: Andantino

Var. III: Allegro

Var. IV: Tempo I

Var. V: Allegro con spirito

6th Theme and Variations

Theme: Moderato

Var. I: Moderato

Var. II: Poco più mosso

Var. III (Minore): Largo

Var. IV (Maggiore): Allegretto

Var. V: Allegro

THEMES AND VARIATIONS *Section II*

7th Theme and Variations

Theme: Allegro innocente

Var. I: Grazioso

Var. II: Andantino

Var. III: Andante

Var. IV (Minore): Adagietto

Var. V (Maggiore): Allegretto

8th Theme and Variations

Theme: Lento

Var. I: Un poco più mosso

Var. II: Andantino

Var. III: Allegretto

Var. IV (Maggiore): Adagio

Var. V (Minore): Allegro gioviale

Var. VI: Allegro

9th Theme and Variations

Theme: Moderato

10th Theme and Variations

Theme: Adagietto

Var. I: Alla marcia

Var. II: Allegretto

Var. III: Allegro misterioso

Var. IV (Maggiore): Largo e cantabile

Var. V (Minore): Valse brillante

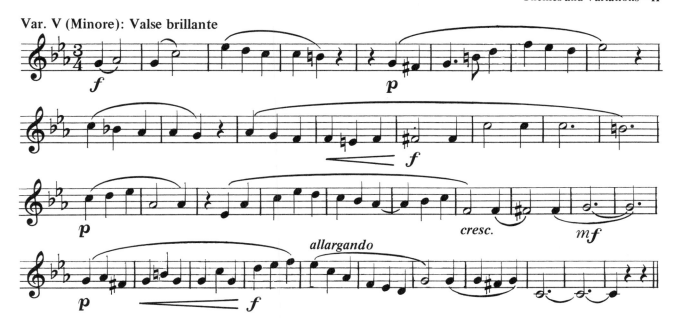

11th Theme and Variations

Theme: Allegretto gioviale

Var. I: Andantino

Var. II: Allegro ma non troppo

Var. III: Adagietto

Var. IV (Minore): Un poco agitato

Var. V (Maggiore): Allegro con brio

THEMES AND VARIATIONS *Section III*

12th Theme and Variations

Var. VI: Allegro

13th Theme and Variations

Theme: Allegretto grazioso

Var. I:

Var. II (Minore): Larghetto

14th Theme and Variations

Theme: Andante

Var. I: Andantino

Var. II: Allegro appassionato

Var. III (Maggiore): Andante tranquillo

Var. IV (Minore): Allegretto

Var. V: Vivace

15th Theme and Variations *

Theme: Jolly

Var. I: Fast

*For review of Modes, see p. 53.

Var. II: Slowly

Var. III: Lively

16th Theme and Variations

Theme: Andante cantabile

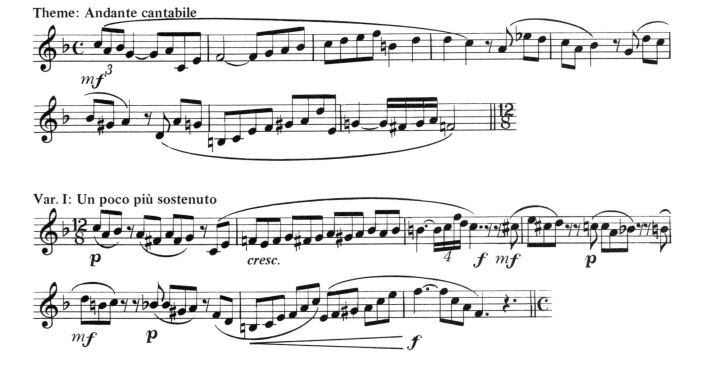

Var. I: Un poco più sostenuto

Var. II: Allegro

Var. III: Allegro deciso

Var. IV: Poco adagio

Var. V: Allegro spiritoso

THEMES AND VARIATIONS   *Section IV*

17th Theme and Variations

Theme: Vivace

Var. I: Allegretto

Var. II: Andantino

Var. III: Un poco sostenuto

Var. IV (Maggiore): Allegro

18th Theme and Variations

Theme: Allegretto

Var. I: Andante

Var. II: Grazioso

Var. III (Minore): Allegro

Var. IV (Maggiore): Andantino cantabile

Var. V: Moderato

Var. VI: Allegro

19th Theme and Variations

Theme: Andante

Var. I:

Var. II (Maggiore): Un poco meno mosso

Var. III (Minore) Moderato

Var. IV: Allegro

molto rit.

20th Theme and Variations

Theme: Allegro deciso

Var. I: Allegretto

Var. II: Allegro

Var. III (Minore): Moderato

Var. IV (Maggiore): Presto

253

Chapter Five

THEMES AND VARIATIONS FOR VOICE AND PIANO

These exercises provide further opportunity for combining voice and piano. Variation procedures illustrate a rich variety of piano textures, harmony, and rhythms in support of the vocal lines. Chapter Five includes a wide range of styles including Baroque, Classical, Romantic, Impressionist, Twentieth-century, jazz, and popular music.

THEMES AND VARIATIONS FOR VOICE AND PIANO
Section I

1st Theme and Variations

Theme: Allegro

Var. I: Allegro

sempre staccato

Var. II: Andante

Var. III: Allegro giocoso

Var. IV: Allegro molto

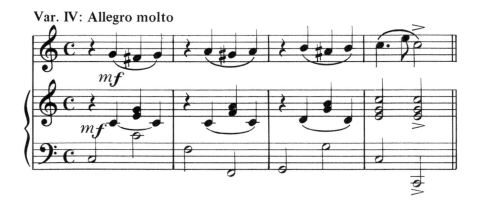

2nd Theme and Variations

Theme: Moderato

Var. I: Andantino

Var. II: March

Var. III: Allegretto

Var. IV: Allegro

Var. V: Andante (Minore)

3rd Theme and Variations

Theme: Allegro deciso

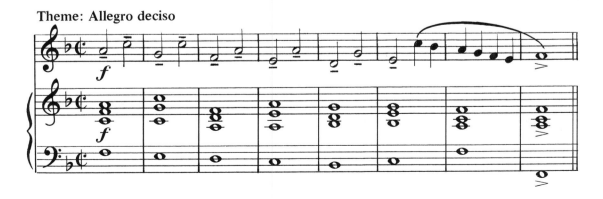

257

Var. I: Allegretto

Var. II: Moderato

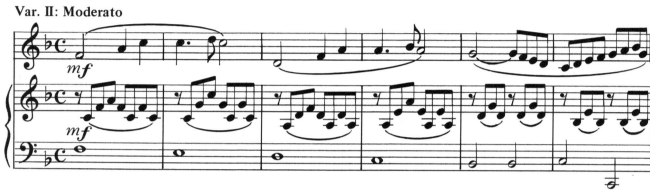

Var. III: Presto

Var. IV: March

4th Theme and Variations

Theme: Andante sostenuto

Var. I: Moderato

Var. II: Adagio

Var. III: Allegro

Var. IV: Allegro

Var. V: Moderato

THEMES AND VARIATIONS FOR VOICE AND PIANO
Section II

5th Theme and Variations

Theme: Moderato

Var. I: Moderato

Var. II: Allegro

Var. III: Allegro

Var. IV: Andante

Var. V: Allegro tranquillo

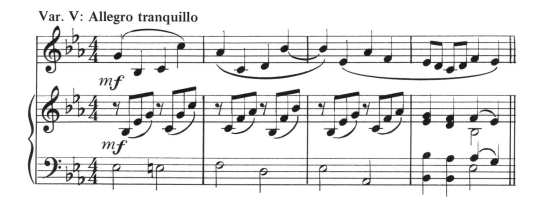

6th Theme and Variations

Theme: Mesto

Var. I: Andante

Var. II: Moderato

Var. III: Andantino

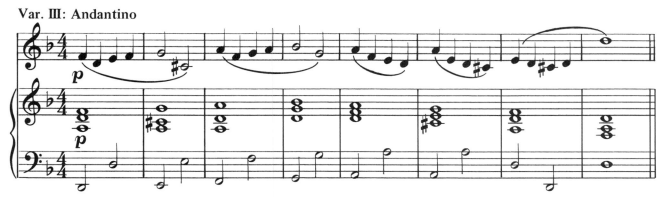

Var. IV: Allegretto

Var. V: Lento

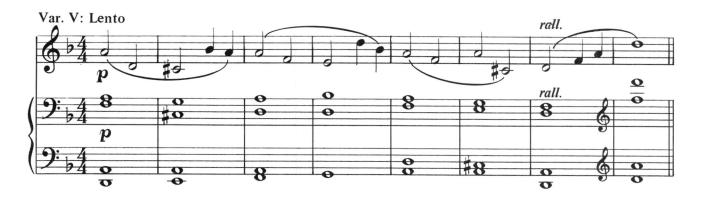

7th Theme and Variations

Theme: Allegro grazioso

Var. I: Allegro

Var. II: Adagio

Var. III: Allegro gioviale

Var. IV: Moderato

Var. V: Allegro

8th Theme and Variations

Theme: Allegro

Var. I: Allegro

Var. II: Moderato

Var. III: Andante espressivo

Var. IV: Allegro

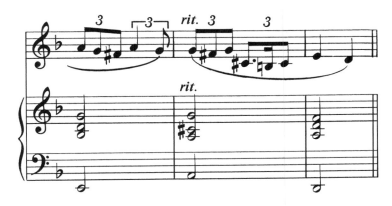

THEMES AND VARIATIONS FOR VOICE AND PIANO
Section III

9th Theme and Variations

Theme: Allegro grazioso

Var. I: Moderato

Var. II: Gioviale

Var. III: Cantabile

Var. IV: Andante espressivo

Var. V: Brillante

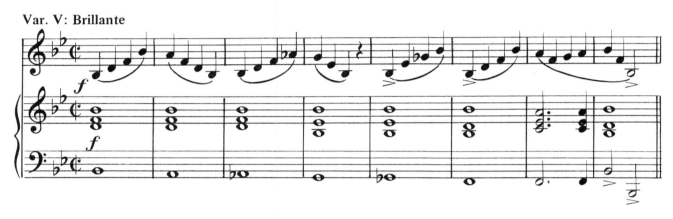

10th Theme and Variations

Theme: Allegro

Var. I: Moderato

Var. II: Lento

Var. III: Adagio

Var. IV: Allegro non troppo

11th Theme and Variations

Var. IV: Moderately fast

Var. V: Jazz waltz

12th Theme and Variations

Theme: Ruhig

Var. I: Walzer

Var. II: Lebhaft

Var. III: Ziemlich langsam

Var. IV: Walzer

Var. V: Ruhig

13th Theme and Variations

Theme: Slow and hymnlike

Var. I: Slow and solemn

Var. II: Lively

Var. III: Fast

Var. IV: Very slow

Var. V: Slow and solemn

14th Theme and Variations

Theme: Andantino

Var. I: Allegretto

Var. II: Allegro

Var. III: Moderato

Var. IV: Allegro

Var. V: Presto

15th Theme and Variations

Theme: Slow and sustained

Var. I: Moderato

Var. II: Andante espressivo

Var. III: Gioviale

Var. IV: L'istesso tempo

Var. V: Innocente

16th Theme and Variations

Theme: Appassionato

Var. I: Allegro

Var. II: Adagio

Var. III: Allegretto

Var. IV: Moderato

Var. V: Allegro grazioso

THEMES AND VARIATIONS FOR VOICE AND PIANO
Section IV

17th Theme and Variations

Theme: Very stately

Var. I: Calmly

Var. II: Slow and expressively

Var. III: Agitated

Var. IV: Very relaxed

Var. V: Mournfully

18th Theme and Variations

Theme: Slow blues

Var. I: Jazz waltz (In one)

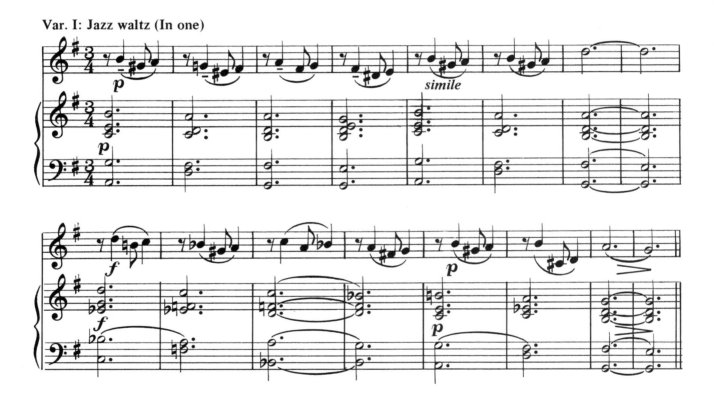

Var. II: Flowing

Var. III: With energy

Var. IV: With excitement

19th Theme and Variations

Theme: Playfully

Var. I: Slow

Var. II: Agitated

Var. III: Slow and solemn

Var. IV: Slow and expressively

20th Theme and Variations

Theme: Adagio sostenuto

Var. I: Grave

Var. II: Piacevole

Var. III: Adagio

Var. IV: Funerale

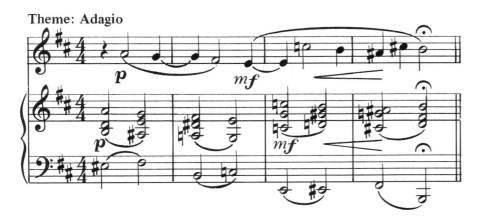
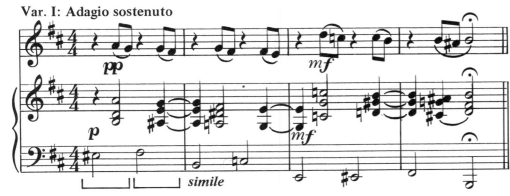

21st Theme and Variations

Theme: Adagio

Var. I: Adagio sostenuto

Var. II: Moderato

Var. III: Piacevole

287

Var. IV: Allegro giocoso

Var. V: Pastorale

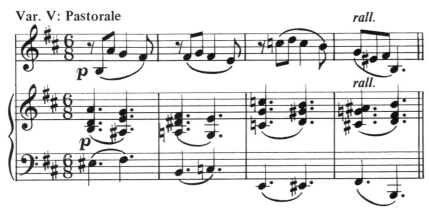

22nd Theme and Variations

Theme: Andante

Var. I: Moderato

Var. II: Allegretto

Var. III: Andante

Var. IV: Allegro (in one)

Var. V: Maestoso

23rd Theme and Variations

Theme: Lent

Var. I: Modéré

Var. II: Gracieux

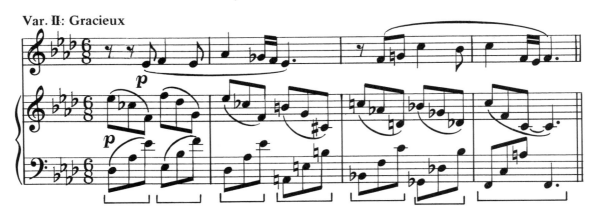

Var. III: Léger

Var. IV: Lentement

Var. V: Gracieux

SUPPLEMENTARY EXERCISES

These drills are designed to focus upon various technical problems. Part I is concerned principally with problems of intonation and the development of the sense of key. Part II concentrates upon problems involving chromaticism. Both parts also contain rhythmic patterns arranged in order of increasing complexity. We suggest that the student first learn an exercise slowly and accurately, then increase the speed as much as possible.

SUPPLEMENTARY EXERCISES *Part I*

Exercises for Use with Sections I and II

Exercises 10–13 are designed to show similarities and differences between the major and minor modes.

67.

68.

69.

70.

71.

72.

SUPPLEMENTARY EXERCISES *Part II*

Exercises for Use with Sections III and IV

81. Ionian mode (major scale)

82. Aeolian mode (natural minor scale)

83. Harmonic minor scale

84. Melodic minor scale

85.   Dorian mode

86.   Mixolydian mode

87.   Phrygian mode

88.   Locrian mode

89.   Lydian mode

90.   Whole tone scale

91.   Chromatic scale

92 a.   Whole-tone and Chromatic scale

92b.   Chromatic and Whole-tone scale

93.

94.

129.

130.

131.

132. **Rhythmic Variations on a Tone Row**

a. **Moderato**

b. **Andante**

c. **Allegro**

d. **Presto**

Appendix I

GLOSSARY OF MUSICAL TERMS

ALL TERMS ARE ITALIAN UNLESS OTHERWISE NOTED. ABBREVIATIONS ARE GIVEN IN PARENTHESES.

Accelerando (accel.), gradually getting faster

Acciaccatura, a short appoggiatura

Adagietto, somewhat faster than adagio

Adagio, slow (slower than andante, faster than largo

Affetto, tenderness

Affettuoso, tender

Agitato, agitated

Al fine, to the end

Alla, to the, at the, in the style of

Allargando, getting slower (crescendo often implied)

Allegretto, moderately fast (slower than allegro, faster than andante)

Allegro, fast, cheerful

All'ottava (8va), at the octave

Amabile, with love

Andante, moderately slow (slower than allegretto, faster than adagio)

Andantino, in modern usage, somewhat faster than andante; in older usage, somewhat slower than andante

Anima, spirit

Animato, animated, spirited

Animé, Fr., animated, spirited

Appassionato, impassioned, intense

Appoggiatura, a melodic ornament; of the many types there are two main classifications: the *accented (long) appoggiatura* and the *short appoggiatura* (grace note). The first, written as a small note, is accented and borrows time value from the note it precedes. The second is usually written as a small eighth or sixteenth note with a slanting stroke through the flag and stem. It is executed quickly, so that the accent falls on the melody note it precedes.

Arietta, a small aria

Assai, very

Assez, Fr., fairly

A tempo, in the original speed

Attacca, attack or begin what follows without pause

Ausdrucksvoll, Ger., expressive

Avec, Fr., with

Ballando, dancing

Ben, well, very

Berceuse, Fr., lullaby

Bewegt, Ger., rather fast, agitated

Breit, Ger., broad, stately

Brillante, brilliant, sparkling

Brio, sprightliness, spirit

Calando, decreasing in both dynamics and tempo

Calma, Calmo, calm, tranquil

Calore, warmth, passion

Cantabile, in a singing or vocal style

Colla voce, literally "with the voice," meaning that the accompanist should follow the free rhythm used by the singer.

Comodo, at a leisurely, convenient pace

Con, with

Crescendo (cresc.), increasing in volume of sound

315

Da capo (D. C.), from the beginning

Da capo al fine, repeat from the beginning to the end; that is, to the place where *fine* is written

Dal segno al fine, repeat from the sign to the end; that is, to the place where *fine* is written

Deciso, decisive, bold

Decrescendo (decresc.), decreasing in volume sound

Del, of the

Détaché, Fr., detached

Di, of

Diminuendo (dim.), decreasing in volume of sound

Dolce, sweet (*soft* is also implied)

Doux, Fr., sweet (*soft* is also implied)

Doucement, Fr., sweet (*soft* is also implied)

E, ed, and

Eco, echo

Einfach, Ger., simple

Empfindung, Ger., expression

En allant, Fr., moving, flowing

Energico, energetic

Espressione, expression

Et, Fr., and

Espressivo (espr.), expressive

Etwas, Ger., somewhat

Expressif, Fr., expressive

Feierlich, Ger., solemn

Fine, end

Fliessend, Ger., flowing

Force, Fr., strength, force

Forte (f), loud

Fortissimo (ff), very loud

Frisch, Ger., brisk, lively

Fröhlich, Ger., joyous, gay

Funebre, funereal

Fuoco, fire

Gai, Fr., gay

Gaio, gay

Galop, Fr., a lively round-dance in duple meter

Gavotte, Fr., a French dance generally in common time, strongly accented, beginning on the third beat

Gedehnt, Ger., extended, sustained

Geshwind, Ger., quick

Gigue, Fr., a very fast dance of English origin in triple or sextuple meter

Giocoso, playful

Gioviale, jovial

Giusto, exact

Gracieux, Fr., graceful

Grave, very slow, solemn (generally indicates the slowest tempo)

Grazia, grace

Grazioso, graceful

Il più, the most

Im Zeitmass, Ger., in the original speed

Innig, Ger., heartfelt, ardent

Innocente, unaffected, artless

Kraft, Ger., strength

Kräftig, Ger., strong, robust

La, It. and Fr., the

Ländler, Ger., a country dance in triple meter

Langsam, Ger., slow

Larghetto, not as slow as largo

Largo, slow, broad

Lebhaft, Ger., lively, animated

Legato, to be performed with no interruption between tones; in a smooth and connected manner

Léger, Fr., light

Leggiero (also *Leggero*), light, delicate

Lent, Fr., slow

Lentement, Fr., slowly

Lento, slow; not as slow as adagio

L'istesso tempo, in the same tempo as the previous section

Lunatico, performed in the spirit of lunacy

Ma, but

Maestoso, majestic, dignified

Maggiore, major (referring to mode)

Mais, Fr., but

Marcato, marked, with emphasis

Marcia, march

Marziale, martial

Mässig, Ger., moderate

Mazurka, Polish national dance in triple meter

Meno, less

Mesto, sad, mournful

Mezzo forte (mf), moderately loud

Mezzo piano (mp), moderately soft

Minore, minor (referring to mode)

Minuetto, minuet (moderately slow dance in triple meter)

Misterioso, mysterious

Mit, Ger., with

Moderato, moderate (slower than allegro, faster than andante)

Modéré, Fr., moderate (slower than allegro, faster than andante)

Möglich, Ger., possible

Molto, much, very

Morendo, dying away

Mosso, in motion (*più mosso*, faster; *meno mosso*, slower)

Moto, motion

Mouvement, Fr., motion, tempo, movement

Munter, Ger., lively

Nicht, Ger., not

Niente, nothing

Non, not

Ongarese, Hungarian

Pas, Fr., not

Pastorale, pastoral

Perdendosi, gradually fading away

Pesante, heavy, ponderous

Peu, Fr., little

Piacevole, pleasant, graceful

Piano (p), soft

Pianissimo (pp), very soft

Più, more

Plus, Fr., more

Poco, little

Poco a poco, little by little, gradually

Pomposo, pompous

Possibile, possible

Pressez, Fr., press forward

Presto, very fast (faster than allegro)

Quasi, almost, nearly

Rallentando (rall.), gradually growing slower

Rasch, Ger., fast

Recitativo, sung in a declamatory manner

Retenu, Fr., held back

Rigore, strictness

Risoluto, firm, resolute

Ritardando (rit.), gradually growing slower

Ritenuto (riten.), held back

Ritmico, rhythmically

Rubato, literally, stolen; the term indicates freedom and flexibility of tempo so that the requirements of musical expression can be met

Ruhig, Ger., calm, tranquil

Saltarello, a lively dance of Italian origin, often in $\frac{9}{8}$

Scherzando, light, playful

Scherzo, a fast piece in triple meter

Scherzoso, jesting, playful

Schnell, Ger., fast

Seconda, second

Sehr, Ger., very

Semplice, simple, unaffected

Sempre, always

Sentimentale, It. and Fr., with sentiment

Senza fretta, without haste

Sforzando (sf, sfz), with force, accented

Siciliano, a moderately slow dance of pastoral character in $\frac{12}{8}$ or $\frac{6}{8}$ time

Simile, alike, in like manner

So, Ger., as

Sostenuto, sustained

Sotto voce, softly, with subdued voice

Spirito, spirit

Spiritoso, with spirit, animated

Staccato, detached

Stark, Ger., strong, vigorous

Stringendo, pressing forward

Subito (sub.), suddenly

Tanto, so much

Tarantella, a lively dance of Italian origin, usually in $\frac{6}{8}$

Tempo, time; refers to rate of motion

Tempo primo (Tempo I), in the original speed

Teneramente, tenderly, delicately

Tranquillo, tranquil

Très, Fr., very

Triste, It. and Fr., sad

Trop, Fr., too much, too

Troppo, too much, too

Un, It. and Fr., a

Und, Ger., and

Valse, Fr., waltz

Valzer, waltz

Vif, Fr., lively

Glossary

Vite, Fr., quickly
Vivace, lively, quick
Vivo, lively, animated
Volta, turn or time

Walzer, Ger., waltz
Wie, Ger., as

Zart, Ger., tender, soft
Zeitmass, Ger., tempo
Ziemlich, Ger., somewhat, rather
Zu, Ger., too, to, by
Zuvor, Ger., previously
Zurückhalten, Ger., to hold back, to retard

Appendix II

SOME FREQUENTLY USED MUSICAL SIGNS

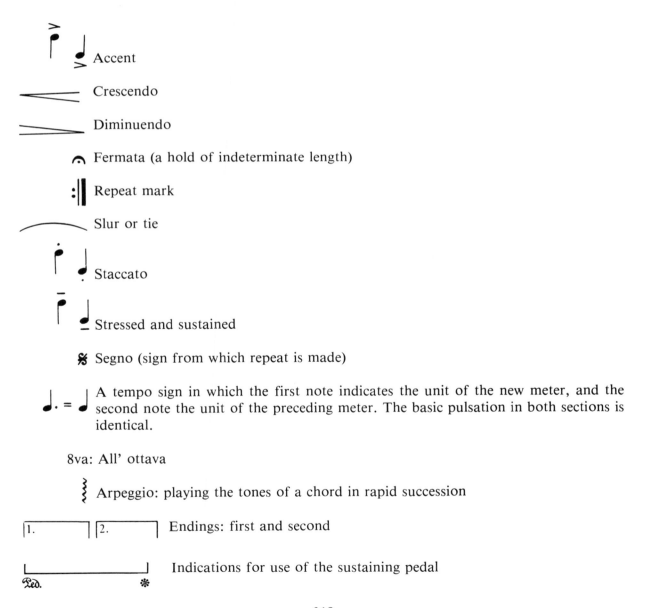

Accent

Crescendo

Diminuendo

Fermata (a hold of indeterminate length)

Repeat mark

Slur or tie

Staccato

Stressed and sustained

Segno (sign from which repeat is made)

A tempo sign in which the first note indicates the unit of the new meter, and the second note the unit of the preceding meter. The basic pulsation in both sections is identical.

8va: All' ottava

Arpeggio: playing the tones of a chord in rapid succession

Endings: first and second

Indications for use of the sustaining pedal

DATE DUE